Acting Edition

Inspired by True Events

by Ryan Spahn

‖SAMUEL FRENCH‖

Copyright © 2025 by Ryan Spahn
All Rights Reserved

INSPIRED BY TRUE EVENTS is fully protected under the copyright laws of the United States of America, the British Commonwealth, including Canada, and all member countries of the Berne Convention for the Protection of Literary and Artistic Works, the Universal Copyright Convention, and/or the World Trade Organization conforming to the Agreement on Trade Related Aspects of Intellectual Property Rights. All rights, including professional and amateur stage productions, recitation, lecturing, public reading, motion picture, radio broadcasting, television, online/digital production, and the rights of translation into foreign languages are strictly reserved.

ISBN 978-0-573-71204-3

www.concordtheatricals.com
www.concordtheatricals.co.uk

FOR PRODUCTION INQUIRIES

UNITED STATES AND CANADA
info@concordtheatricals.com
1-866-979-0447

UNITED KINGDOM AND EUROPE
licensing@concordtheatricals.co.uk
020-7054-7298

Each title is subject to availability from Concord Theatricals Corp., depending upon country of performance. Please be aware that *INSPIRED BY TRUE EVENTS* may not be licensed by Concord Theatricals Corp. in your territory. Professional and amateur producers should contact the nearest Concord Theatricals Corp. office or licensing partner to verify availability.

CAUTION: Professional and amateur producers are hereby warned that *INSPIRED BY TRUE EVENTS* is subject to a licensing fee. The purchase, renting, lending or use of this book does not constitute a license to perform this title(s), which license must be obtained from Concord Theatricals Corp. prior to any performance. Performance of this title(s) without a license is a violation of federal law and may subject the producer and/or presenter of such performances to civil penalties. Both amateurs and professionals considering a production are strongly advised to apply to the appropriate agent before starting rehearsals, advertising, or booking a theatre. A licensing fee must be paid whether the title(s) is presented for charity or gain and whether or not admission is charged. Professional/Stock licensing fees are quoted upon application to Concord Theatricals Corp.

This work is published by Samuel French, an imprint of Concord Theatricals Corp.

No one shall make any changes in this title(s) for the purpose of production. No part of this book may be reproduced, stored in a retrieval system, scanned, uploaded, or transmitted in any form, by any means, now known or yet to be invented, including mechanical, electronic, digital, photocopying, recording, videotaping, or otherwise, without the prior written permission of the publisher. No one shall share this title(s), or any part of this title(s), through any social media or file hosting websites.

For all inquiries regarding motion picture, television, online/digital and other media rights, please contact Concord Theatricals Corp.

MUSIC AND THIRD-PARTY MATERIALS USE NOTE

Licensees are solely responsible for obtaining formal written permission from copyright owners to use copyrighted music and/or other copyrighted third-party materials (e.g. artworks, logos) in the performance of this play and are strongly cautioned to do so. If no such permission is obtained by the licensee, then the licensee must use only original music and materials that the licensee owns and controls. Licensees are solely responsible and liable for clearances of all third-party copyrighted materials, including without limitation music, and shall indemnify the copyright owners of the play(s) and their licensing agent, Concord Theatricals Corp., against any costs, expenses, losses and liabilities arising from the use of such copyrighted third-party materials by licensees. For music, please contact the appropriate music licensing authority in your territory for the rights to any incidental music.

IMPORTANT BILLING AND CREDIT REQUIREMENTS

If you have obtained performance rights to this title, please refer to your licensing agreement for important billing and credit requirements.

INSPIRED BY TRUE EVENTS was originally produced by Out of the Box Theatrics (Elizabeth Flemming, Producing Artistic Director) at Theater 154 in New York City on July 10th, 2024. The production was directed by Knud Adams, with set design by Lindsay G. Fuori, costume design by Siena Zoë Allen, sound design by Peter Mills Weiss, lighting design by Paige Seber, and prop design by Sean Frank. The production stage manager was Jakob W. Plummer, and the assistant stage manager was Giselle Raphaela. The production manager was Sajari Hume. The cast was as follows:

MARY . . . . Dana Scurlock
COLIN . . . . Jack DiFalco
EILEEN . . . . Mallory Portnoy
ROBERT . . . . Lou Liberatore
CHRISTINA (OFFSTAGE VOICE) . . . . Giselle Raphaela

INSPIRED BY TRUE EVENTS received development workshops with New York Stage and Film, the Vineyard Theatre, and Ensemble Studio Theatre.

While inspired by true events, any resemblance to actual events or persons, living or dead, is purely coincidental.

CHARACTERS

MARY – (40s) Stage Manager.
COLIN – (20s) Actor.
EILEEN – (30s) Actor. Wears a pregnant belly in the scenes on the monitor.
ROBERT – (50s) Actor.
VARIOUS OFFSTAGE VOICES –
Christina
Female Cop
Male Cop

SETTING

The green room of a community theatre
in downtown Rochester, New York.

TIME

7:10 p.m.

PRODUCTION NOTE

In the original production, a live video feed on a TV monitor displayed the play-within-the-play in real time from another location inside the building. For future productions, this element can be adapted as needed – using pre-recorded video or even an audio-only feed – depending on budget and venue constraints.

(The green room of a community theatre in downtown Rochester, New York. 7:10 p.m.)

(A used rug lies under a large communal table. In the corner, a TV monitor hangs. There's a dirty couch, vending machine, coffee maker, water station, and recycling. All the general stuff you'd find in an old community theatre.)

(Against the wall, there is a long mirror, chairs, and a few dressing stations. Above are ceiling and wall vents. They are all around.)

(The stage manager, **MARY***, 40, enters through the side door. She's carrying a tote embroidered with "Uptown Theatre: Kicking Ass For 15 Seasons." She dumps a stack of papers into the recycling bin and turns on a few old lamps. There's a radio nearby, which she turns on. She shuffles stations until she finds something relaxing.* This is her time.)*

*(***MARY*** collects glasses, dishes, and leftover booze from last night's opening night party. She preps coffee. Once finished, she pours herself a cup and sits. She looks through her script-binder. The play is called* When Tragedy Comes Home *by Beth Riley.)*

(Through an intercom...)

---

* A license to produce *Inspired by True Events* does not include a performance license for any third-party or copyrighted recordings. Licensees should create their own.

CHRISTINA. *(Offstage, from the intercom, extremely broken up.)* Check, one-two. Ahhh. Check, shit. Is this even working? Ahhh. Can anyone hear me? Hello?

>*(Silence.)*

MARY. *(Looking up, annoyed.)* Really, Christina?

>*(**MARY** exits down the hall that leads to the rest of the theatre.)*

>*(After a few moments, **COLIN**, 25 and disheveled, appears from a dressing room. He sits, worn out.)*

>*(The intercom comes back on...)*

>*(**MARY** speaks offstage, from the intercom.)*

You press / this.

CHRISTINA. *(From the intercom.)* / Oh. I see.

MARY. And you have to hold it down the entire time / you're talking.

CHRISTINA. Oh. Right. I wasn't doing / that.

MARY. Yes, I / know.

CHRISTINA. I thought I was supposed to –

>*(The intercom goes out.)*

>*(After a moment, **MARY** enters the green room.)*

MARY. Oh, hey Colin.

COLIN. *(A smile.)* Hey, Mary.

MARY. When did you get here?

COLIN. A few minutes ago.

MARY. Okay.

>   *(Beat.)*

Did Christina let you in?

>   *(Beat.)*

COLIN. Betty and John did. They were folding programs.

MARY. Oh, wonderful. We're gonna need extra programs this weekend.

(Huge smile.) Wasn't opening so fun?

>   *(**COLIN** nods in agreement.)*

I know you had that prop issue and I'm sorry. That's on me. Did you get my text? A new gun should be here next week, but until then, we're gonna have to use the sound effect. I personally think it worked just as well, didn't you?

>   *(**COLIN** shrugs. He's distant, out of it.)*

The audience was still scared, which is all Tina was really going for.

>   *(**COLIN** nods.)*

I hope it didn't throw you. Did it?

>   *(Beat.)*

Your gun not working? Did it mess you up?

COLIN. No.

MARY. Good.

>   *(Beat.)*

You okay?

COLIN. *(Beat.)* Yes.

MARY. Hm.

MARY. *(Changing gears, huge smile.)* Well, I was so proud of y'all. Did y'all feel proud?

> *(COLIN nods, agreeing.)*

COLIN. *(Beat.)* I just need coffee.

MARY. I put a fresh pot on, so have at it.

> *(COLIN heads to the coffee maker.)*

COLIN. Why aren't you up in the booth?

MARY. What was that, honey?

COLIN. *(A little louder.)* Why aren't you in the theatre?

MARY. Christina's calling the show. I told you. She's covering while I'm at the wedding.

> *(COLIN finds some cream for his coffee. MARY studies him, curious.)*

> *(Suddenly, a terrifyingly loud noise comes from inside the wall. Something falls. It's startling, making clanking noises. It lands with a thud.)*

(Yelling.) Oh god!!

COLIN. Shit.

> *(They both stare at the vent. The one that's closest to the ground.)*

MARY. What was that?

> *(COLIN shrugs, uneasy.)*

Do you think it was the mice? Oh lord, do you think one of them crawled inside and got trapped and just fell? I'm gonna be sick.

(**MARY** *heads towards the vent.*)

COLIN. Don't open it.

MARY. I'm just giving it a look.

(*Peeking into the vent.*)

When we had the outbreak last fall, one of them ran straight up my leg.

(*Beat, sniffing.*)

Ugh... Is that mold? That better not be black mold.

(*Beat.*)

I don't see anything.

(**MARY** *returns to the table.*)

(*To herself, mumbling.*) I am not dealing with this. No. That shit is Todd's problem. I'm in too good a mood to let those little fuckers ruin it.

(*Without saying much,* **COLIN** *oddly stalks to the dressing room.*)

(*A song* **MARY** *loves comes on the radio. She turns it up and dances around. Sings, even.**)

(*Moments later,* **COLIN** *appears. He stares at* **MARY**. *She tries to dance with him, but he doesn't play along.*)

You're missing out on all this.

(**MARY** *continues. After nothing from* **COLIN**, *she reluctantly turns the music down.*)

---

* A license to produce *Inspired by True Events* does not include a performance license for any third-party or copyrighted music. Licensees should create an original composition or use music in the public domain. For further information, please see the Music and Third-Party Materials Use Note on page iii.

MARY. Someone's in a mood.

> (**MARY** *returns to her work.*)
>
> (*After a long, long while of nobody talking...*)

(*Laughing.*) Oh, you'll love this. You know my pull-out couch?

COLIN. Yeah.

MARY. Oh, wait, did I tell you that Nia's coming back with me? After the wedding?

COLIN. No.

MARY. Well, she is and she will *insist* on seeing you.

> (**COLIN** *nods.*)

So, I wake up this morning, turn on my phone, and I see this email from Nia with the subject line "SOS." Of course, I start freaking out, I'm thinking our mother must have died, but Nia's just bitching about how "she refuses to sleep on my pull-out" and how I need to "buy her a futon." So I spend the entire afternoon driving from mattress store to mattress store hoping to find something under three hundred dollars. Thankfully I found something that wasn't too expensive, which of course Nia will not repay me for.

COLIN. (*Beat.*) Return it.

MARY. Return what?

COLIN. The futon. The mattress. After she leaves.

MARY. It will be used.

COLIN. (*Mumbling.*) I'd need the money.

> (*Silence falls.*)

MARY. You sure you're okay? You're usually much more chatty.

(Beat.)

So, what did *you* think of opening?

(COLIN shrugs.)

Oh, a standing "O" isn't good enough for you? How about that second curtain call?

(COLIN shrugs again.)

Give me a break. People went crazy. Rhonda from the Java Detour said it was the greatest show she'd ever seen us do, and that's including our *12 Angry Jurors*.

(Beat.)

Did Rhonda talk to you at the party last night?

(Dead silence. COLIN is lost in thought.)

(Then –)

COLIN. *(Beat.)* No.

(MARY heads back to her laptop.)

MARY. She was probably too nervous. Rhonda has a little crush on you, FYI.

(Then, serious work-mode.) Oh, and I know everyone was excited, but our show was very long last night.

COLIN. Okay.

MARY. It was mostly in the final scene. It was dragging.

COLIN. I'm not in the final scene.

MARY. I know.

COLIN. I just do the opening speech.

MARY. I know, honey, but some people have been taking liberties.

COLIN. Then you should talk to those people.

MARY. I have texted with Eileen and Robert, but I'm also speaking to you. This is an ensemble show. We have been adding minutes since we started having audiences.

COLIN. *(Growing annoyed.) Minutes?*

MARY. I'm just letting you – *and them* – know in case anyone's developing a pattern.

COLIN. Got it! No patterns!

MARY. Oh, you got an attitude?

COLIN. *(Abrasive, violent.) Just leave me the fuck alone, Mary!! You are not my fucking mother!!!*

> *(**COLIN** explodes. It's sudden. Loud.)*

> *(**MARY** stands, a bit rattled, but plays it cool.)*

MARY. No need to yell.

> *(Beat.)*

Have some respect.

> *(**COLIN** nods. **MARY** refills her coffee, trying to make light of his behavior, but she's eyeing him.)*

(To herself, mumbling.) All y'all do is mess around like this play is your damn hobby. I know it's only $16/hour, but that's a huge increase, so instead of being grateful, you just do whatever you want, making up dialogue, making me out to be the bad guy.

> *(**COLIN** continues to breathe, slowly.)*

> *(Beat.)*

(Tentative.) Honey?

(Beat.)

You're making me nervous.

COLIN. *(Beat.)* I, ah...

(Overwhelmingly emotional.) Claire and I... We broke up.

MARY. Oh no. Colin, I'm sorry.

COLIN. *(A release.)* I, ah... moved out. After the show. I wandered around. All night. Didn't know... where to go.

MARY. Honey, why didn't you just come to me?

> *(**COLIN** shrugs. **MARY** hugs him. Caretaker mode.)*

Oh baby, I'm so sorry.

> *(Silence.)*

> *(**COLIN** calms down. Breathes. Relaxes.)*

COLIN. *(Quietly.)* Thanks.

> *(**MARY** smells something on him.)*

MARY. Ew, Colin. Did you put on deodorant?

(Sniffing.) I think you may need to swipe those pits.

COLIN. I should shower.

MARY. That would be a good idea. For all of our benefits.

> *(Suddenly, there's a strange noise. Coming from the same vent as before. It's loud and bizarre, like fingernails scratching on drywall.)*

> *(But this time, something small rolls out.)*

(Caught off guard.) Oh shit! What the hell is that?

> *(**COLIN** takes a deep breath. He looks unwell.)*

>   *(**MARY** glances at him and then back at the vent. Her instincts flare, something about this whole evening feels not right.)*

MARY. You sure you're okay?

>   *(**COLIN** doesn't respond.)*

COLIN. *(Beat.)* Yes.

>   *(Saving face, **MARY** walks over, slowly, and tentatively bends down to see what rolled out.)*

MARY. Oh thank god, it's just a costume button. I thought that was a roach. Ugh.

>   *(**MARY** inspects. The button has something on it.)*

Ew. It's sticky. Gross.

>   *(**COLIN** grows wary as **MARY** tosses the button into the trash. She washes her hands and grabs her phone.)*

Todd is getting on my last nerve.

(To herself.) This is just so unsanitary. He should sell this damn theatre if he's gonna let it go to shit.

>   *(As **MARY** works out her text to Todd, **COLIN** disappears into the bathroom.)*

(To herself, buried in her text.) I was listening to this podcast, and they were talking about these young, healthy people of the Navajo nation who suddenly were dropping dead from some mysterious sickness. Their lungs were filling with so much fluid that they'd suffocate and nobody knew why. Turns out, it was because there were too many mice in their community. What if something like that happens to us?

(Realizing she's alone.) Oh. You're not even here. I'm just talking to my damn self.

> *(The bathroom shower gets turned on.)*

> *(**MARY** pulls a pizza box from the fridge and microwaves a slice.)*

> *(After several moments, **COLIN** returns. Dripping wet, he wears only a towel.)*

COLIN. Where are our costumes?

MARY. *(Caught off guard.)* Oh, Colin! You're half-naked!

> *(Beat.)*

Eileen took everything to her house because... *Todd!!*

> *(**MARY** walks to the couch and sits. She starts another lengthy text.)*

(To herself, buried in her phone.) One of these days, he's gonna push me too hard, and – just you wait – I will pick up my damn phone, give Todd's wifey a little text, and let her know all about what Todd's been doing on Monday nights. And let me just say, he ain't been going to his bowling league.

(Looking at watch.) We're coming up on half hour, so Eileen should be here soon with the wardrobe.

> *(**COLIN** plops down next to **MARY**.)*

> *(Beat.)*

COLIN. I didn't mean to yell.

> *(Beat.)*

MARY. *(Imparting wisdom.)* You're sad. And that's hard. But, it won't always feel like this. It just takes time, sweetie.

(**COLIN** *nods.*)

MARY. And, you're right, I'm *not* your mom.

COLIN. That's not what / I meant.

MARY. I know, but sometimes I *can* cross a line. I shouldn't.

(*Beat.*)

(*Tactful.*) Um... Did your dad try to contact you?

COLIN. (*Hardened.*) No.

MARY. (*Beat, trying to understand.*) Can I ask what happened? With Claire?

(**COLIN** *stares off.*)

(*Long beat. Then –*)

COLIN. I was gonna propose.

MARY. You were?

COLIN. I was, uh, saving to buy her a ring. I don't have a lot of money, so it was gonna be a cubic zirconia.

(*Beat.*)

And, um...

(*Beat.*)

She belittles me.

(*Silence.* **COLIN** *tenses, loses his train of thought.* **MARY** *studies him.*)

(*Beat.*)

MARY. Did you take your meds?

(**COLIN** *says nothing.*)

(*Beat.*)

COLIN. I will right now.

*(**COLIN** goes to the dressing room.)*

(From offstage –)

When I got home, I was drunk and Claire was like, "Did you pay for your own booze?" And I was like, "The theatre did." And then Claire was like, "You take advantage of people." And then I was like, "It was opening. Why the fuck were you not there?" And... um... We were screaming... I can't even... Then she was like, "You're just like your dad."

*(**MARY** nods, putting it all together.)*

(Beat.)

I had just asked my neighbor if I could borrow some money, to buy her a ring, and then she throws that dad shit in my face?

*(**COLIN** appears, swallowing a few pills.)*

(Beat.)

Maybe Claire is right. Maybe I am like my dad.

*(**MARY** turns to him.)*

MARY. No. She was hurt and so she said something she knew would hurt you. If Claire's gonna be like that, I'll make sure she never gets an acting job here again. How about that?

*(**COLIN** blinks, doesn't say much.)*

Listen, honey. You're the star of a hit play. Did you read our reviews? The word "transcendent" was used. Mmmm-hmmm. Describing *your* performance. I've read every review for every show we've done, and "transcendent" has never been attributed to anyone's performance. Ever.

MARY. *(Stage manager mode.)* Try to nap. Close your eyes. Even for a minute. You'll feel better. Maybe eat something.

COLIN. I have a protein bar in my car.

MARY. *(Beat.)* You drove? I thought you walked around all night.

> (**COLIN** *doesn't say anything.*)
>
> *(Then –)*

COLIN. *(Quietly, to himself.)* I don't know what I did.

MARY. *(Beat.)* Um...

> *(Beat.)*

MARY. How about you have some of my leftover meatloaf? It's in the fridge.

COLIN. I can't eat a big meal before a show.

(Rubbing his head.) Man, I definitely drank too much of that green punch.

MARY. Ohhh.

> (**MARY** *grabs some Tylenol from the first aid kit and hands it over to him.*)

(Looking at her watch.) We're at half hour. Don't forget to sign in.

COLIN. Thank you, half.

> (**COLIN** *walks to the sign-in sheet on the wall. There's a sheet of stickers hanging next to it.*)

You got us *Friends* stickers?

MARY. God no. I hate that show. Eileen got 'em.

COLIN. *(Beat.)* I'll be Ross.

(**COLIN** *takes a Ross sticker off the sheet and marks himself "signed-in."*)

MARY. Hey, Colin?

(*A smile.*)

Fuck Claire.

(**COLIN** *wanders into the dressing room.*)

(*Once he's gone,* **MARY** *doesn't move. She looks at the vent.* **MARY** *notices a smudge. Not mold. Something else. She glances at where* **COLIN** *just went. A spidey sense.*)

(**MARY** *picks up her walkie.*)

(*Into the walkie, gossipy.*) Hey Christina.

CHRISTINA. (*Offstage, from the walkie.*) Go for Christina.

MARY. Just a heads up: Colin's going through one of his spells. Do you want me to call the show?

CHRISTINA. I think I'm okay.

MARY. All right.

(*Beat.*)

Oh, and the mice have returned.

CHRISTINA. No. I hate it.

MARY. Oh god, me, too.

(**MARY** *returns to her work, prepping things and checking her watch.*

(*Breaking the silence,* **EILEEN**, *30, comes barreling in. Always complaining, she wears a backpack filled with cardboard tubes, and pushes a bike stacked with laundry.*)

(**MARY** *is startled.*)

EILEEN. I hate people. I love my friends, but I hate / people.

MARY. Hey / Eileen. You missed half hour.

(*Taking the laundry.*) Let me help you.

EILEEN. (*Motor-mouthed.*) Sorry, but the bike lane is there – for a reason! – thank you, half – and yet, these idiots just fling their doors open and I'm barreling down the bike lane, not realizing I'm seconds away from being *doored*. Look at my knees, they're totally fucked. I slammed on my brakes, which thank god I just had fixed, and turned towards the sidewalk to avoid this prick, and of course there were tons of people walking around, and so now I'm weaving through them and end up smashing into a fucking fire hydrant.

(*Looking at her knee.*) Ugh, it's totally fucked.

MARY. Do you need a Band-Aid?

EILEEN. That'd be great.

> (**MARY** *finds a Band-Aid and some ointment, while* **EILEEN** *cleans her knee at the sink.*)

(*Almost laughing, fast.*) So then this driver, who is probably a tourist, wait who am I kidding, we don't have tourists because nothing interesting ever happens in this town. But the idiot didn't even acknowledge what he'd just done. He just, like, shuts his door and drives off. I'm lying face down, could've been dead, but does he give a shit? Nope. God, what a dick.

> (*An underwhelmed* **MARY** *hands* **EILEEN** *the First Aid Kit.*)

(*Applying a Band-Aid.*) Thanks. My meniscus better not be torn. Oh wait, I got his license plate number. I need a pen. Quick, before I forget. Do you see a pen? Mary! Pen, pen, pen!

MARY. *(Handing a pen.)* Here, Eileen, here.

EILEEN. Thanks.

(Writing, trying to remember.) ADL 234... Shit.

> *(Beat.)*

234-something, something. What was the...? Damnit.

> *(Beat.)*

How can a human being look at a person lying on the ground, laundry just flung everywhere, and just leave them?

> *(Beat.)*

What was the...? 234... Ugh, never mind. I can't remember.

> *(**EILEEN** goes to her bike and pulls out laundry from the basket.)*

MARY. *(Re: laundry.)* I really appreciate you doing this.

EILEEN. Somebody had to. Is Todd gonna ever fix our machines?

MARY. I don't know, Eileen.

EILEEN. Ugh. His house is twice as large as mine, so if I'm stuck doing our laundry, then he needs to give me a pay bump.

> *(**EILEEN** leans her bike against the wall.)*

And no, Mary. I'm not leaving my bike in the parking lot. If I'm responsible for schlepping our shit, then I shouldn't be worrying about it being stolen.

MARY. M'kay. I can do the laundry from now on.

EILEEN. You shouldn't be doing it either. You are not the villain. I am not the villain. The men are the villains.

I swear to god, if this ruins my show, I'm writing a formal complaint.

MARY. To who?

EILEEN. Actor's Equity! If this were a union theatre, I would report Todd. They would have a field day if they knew we worked in this squalor. I almost died.

(**EILEEN** *goes to the sign-in sheet.*)

(*Re: the stickers.*) Ooooo nice. My *Friends* sign-in stickers! I'll be Kudrow. Obviously.

(*Suddenly gasping.*) Oh my god.

MARY. What?

EILEEN. Oh, no.

MARY. What, what?

EILEEN. That crowd of people around me was so worried when I was lying on the ground and I should've said, "Come see me in my play."

MARY. (*Simply.*) It wouldn't'a mattered.

EILEEN. That's a very disheartening thing to say. We've been playing to half houses. It's humiliating. If we're a quarter full again, I'm not doing the show.

MARY. Eileen?

(*Playing it cool.*) We're sold out.

EILEEN. What does that mean?

MARY. There are no tickets left.

EILEEN. I know what it means, just what do you mean?

MARY. The box office said it was the biggest response they've ever had after an opening.

EILEEN. Really?

MARY. Yes.

EILEEN. Holy shit!

> (**EILEEN** *excitedly goes to her bike and grabs the cardboard tubes.*)

(Beaming.) Oh my god! I can't believe it! I have to text my husband!

> (**EILEEN** *grabs her phone and texts.*)

MARY. I didn't get a chance to catch up with him last night. How is Brett?

EILEEN. *(Super sincere.)* Aw. Thanks for asking. You know what? He's in a better place. He's moved into a management position, which he says makes him feel like a man again, so we've been talking more seriously about having kids.

(Back to business.) Do you think we'll add more shows?

MARY. Assuming everyone is available and interested.

EILEEN. We're interested. We're interested. Have you told Colin?

MARY. He's not feeling well.

EILEEN. Is he sick?

MARY. He and Claire broke up.

EILEEN. *(Total gossip.)* Was it because she skipped opening? That was fucked up and I'm already not a fan. Actually, I bet she skipped because she didn't wanna have to run into me.

> (**MARY** *just looks at her.*)

What? I got her part. She auditioned, but I got it.

MARY. Okay. Well, he's very upset.

EILEEN. Oh man, Old Town Playhouse is gonna be so pissed when they find out we're a hit. I bet they don't even know what "successful" means. Serves them right for never casting me.

>   *(Beat.)*

(Clutching the tubes.) Okay, before you say "no," hear me out.

MARY. *(Looking at her watch.)* We're at twenty.

EILEEN. Thank you, twenty.

>   (**MARY** *grabs her walkie.*)

MARY. *(Into the walkie, teaching moment.)* Hey Christina.

CHRISTINA. *(Offstage, from the walkie.)* Go for Christina.

MARY. You ready to do the twenty-minute call?

CHRISTINA. Yes.

MARY. Say welcome back and congratulations on your fabulous / opening.

CHRISTINA. *(Super broken-up.)* Welcome back, everyone. And congratulations on your fabulous opening night!

MARY. Say this is your twenty-minute call and please / sign in.

CHRISTINA. I want to remind you that this is your twenty-minute call. If you haven't signed in, please do so.

MARY. Remind everyone that you're calling the / show tonight.

CHRISTINA. I just want to remind you that I am calling the show tonight while Mary is on vacation.

MARY. Tell them about the house / being open.

CHRISTINA. Oh right. House is now open, house is now open.

MARY. Great. That is great.

CHRISTINA. Okay thank you, Mary.

>   *(The intercom chaotically goes out.)*

EILEEN. Let's hope she doesn't fuck things up.

MARY. Don't be a mean girl.

EILEEN. How am I being a mean girl when Christina can't even use the intercom / correctly?

>   *(Suddenly, a horrifyingly loud thud comes from the dressing room. They're both scared.)*

EILEEN & MARY. Ah!!

EILEEN. What the hell was that?!

MARY. I don't know.

>   *(Beat.)*

(Yelling off.) Colin?

>   *(Beat.)*

Hey, Colin?

>   *(Silence.)*

Colin? I'm coming to the dressing room.

COLIN. *(Offstage.)* Don't come in!

(Out of breath.) I'm fine.

MARY. *(Yelling off.)* You sure?

COLIN. Yeah.

MARY. What was that?

>   *(Odd beat.)*

COLIN. Nothing.

MARY. Didn't sound like nothing. I'm coming in there.

(**MARY** *opens the door. From inside the dressing room,* **COLIN** *yanks the door shut.*)

COLIN. *(Offstage, yelling.)* DON'T COME IN HERE!

EILEEN. *(Over it.)* Oh my god.

COLIN. I'm naked.

MARY. You don't have to scream. What was that?

COLIN. The cabinet fell.

MARY. How did it fall?

COLIN. I was standing on it.

MARY. Why were you standing on it?

COLIN. To open the vents. It's hot. I'll be out in a minute. I'm just gonna pick it up.

(*The chaotic sound of furniture being lifted can be heard behind the door.*)

MARY. Do you need help?

COLIN. No.

EILEEN. *(Beat, conspiratorially.)* Do you think he was trying to hurt himself? Because of Claire?

MARY. That's not funny.

(Looking at her watch.) Have you heard anything from Robert? He's never this late.

EILEEN. He hasn't texted.

MARY. Damnit. I'm not a babysitter. You people need to just do your jobs.

(*Beat.*)

(Yelling off.) Hey Colin? Come out here for a second. I'd like to see your face.

COLIN. No.

MARY. Why not?

(Beat.)

COLIN. I'm...ah...

(Beat.)

Is Eileen here?

MARY. Yes.

COLIN. Can you put my costume outside the door?

MARY. Come and get it yourself.

COLIN. I'm totally naked. Do you want to see my dick?

MARY. Not appropriate! Just put your towel back on and come here.

COLIN. Help me, Mary.

(Beat.)

Please?

*(**MARY** reluctantly grabs Colin's costume.)*

MARY. *(Multi-tasking, to herself.)* It's like a hen house. I'll start running things like a union theatre, if that's what you really want, and then we'll see just how much fun it is to work here.

*(**MARY** places Colin's wardrobe.)*

Okay. Everything's there for you.

*(**MARY** gets her phone and dials.)*

*(From offstage, **COLIN** grabs his stack of wardrobe.)*

EILEEN. *(Back to business.)* I know this is ultimately your decision, but just hear me out...

(**EILEEN** *opens her cardboard tubes and spreads out extremely large pieces of paper onto a table.*)

EILEEN. These are our reviews. Let's hang them. In the lobby.

MARY. *(Leaving voicemail, into the phone.)* Hey Todd, it's Mary. One of our leads isn't feeling well and we need to discuss possibly cancelling the show / tonight.

EILEEN. / What?

MARY. Give me a call ASAP.

(**MARY** *hangs up.*)

EILEEN. We cannot cancel.

MARY. Last time he was acting like this, he hit someone during fight call.

EILEEN. That was an isolated incident. Please, Mary. We cannot cancel.

MARY. It's not my decision. It's Todd's.

(Re: the reviews.) And, no, we're not hanging any of those.

EILEEN. Why not? Genuine ask.

MARY. Because, Eileen. Not every actor likes having their reviews plastered around.

EILEEN. If they're good, they don't mind.

MARY. Can we discuss this later?

EILEEN. You're in a mood.

MARY. You know what? I am. I am tired of being taken advantage of.

(Leaving voicemail, into the phone.) Hey Robert, it's Mary. It's almost 7:45. Just wondering where you are. Thanks.

(Hanging up.) See if Robert's called you.

EILEEN. *(Sighing, grabbing phone.)* You didn't listen to anything I –

(Looking at phone.) He hasn't called, but Mary: we have to hang these because then Todd can raise ticket prices and we can use all that extra money to properly fix shit.

MARY. I'm not posting reviews without Todd's consent.

EILEEN. Mary, please.

> *(Beat.)*

(Delicate.) My mom is here tonight.

> (**MARY** *is taken aback.*)

Don't make it a thing.

> *(Beat.)*

MARY. *(Thoughtful.)* We can hang one review. But just one.

EILEEN. Oh thank you, Mary. Let me pick which one. Can I pick which one?

MARY. Sure.

> *(Beat.)*

EILEEN. *(Glancing them all over.)* The Gazette. It's the most generous to all of us, except for that dig about Robert's new toupee. But I blacked that out.

MARY. *(Grabbing it, annoyed.)* Very thoughtful.

> (**MARY** *looks at her watch and turns on the monitor and the TV screen, which plays a video feed of the empty stage.*)
>
> *(Through the speakers, the murmurs of the audience entering and chattering can be heard.)*

MARY. Text me if Robert gets here, will you?

EILEEN. Of course.

MARY. *(Into the walkie, under breath.)* Hey Christina.

CHRISTINA. *(Offstage, from the walkie.)* Go for Christina.

>*(**MARY** walks out.)*

MARY. *(Offstage.)* It's just one thing after another down here, but I'm coming on up...

>*(**EILEEN** gets on a chair and listens to the audience through the speaker.)*

>*(Suddenly, there's that weird scratching noise.)*

EILEEN. *(Grossed out.)* Fucking hell.

>*(**EILEEN** inspects the vent on the wall that **MARY** had inspected earlier.)*

>*(The intercom comes on, which startles **EILEEN**.)*

>*(Beat.)*

CHRISTINA. *(Offstage, from the intercom.)* This is your fifteen / minute –

>*(Offstage, from the intercom, **MARY** side-coaches **CHRISTINA**.)*

MARY. – call.

EILEEN. Thank you, / fifteen.

CHRISTINA. Call. Fifteen minutes till top of / show.

MARY. Fifteen minutes. Right. And now make sure to say thank / you.

CHRISTINA. Fifteen minutes, thank you.

MARY. If that light is flashing then you can't press / it.

CHRISTINA. I know.

MARY. Do you?

> (*MARY and CHRISTINA continue to bicker as the intercom chaotically goes off.*)

EILEEN. (*To herself.*) Wow.

> (*EILEEN stretches. She does a few vocal warm-ups. She practices a song, perhaps for an upcoming audition she's nervous about.**)

> (*After a moment,* **ROBERT***, 50s, hurries in. Terrible toupee and all, he's a total delight.*)

ROBERT. (*Amped up.*) Sorry, sorry, I know, I know, I know – I got behind at work and traffic was insane.

EILEEN. Text Mary you're here because she started to freak.

ROBERT. Really?

EILEEN. Kinda. And we're at fifteen.

ROBERT. Thank you, fifteen. Ugh. My phone died, my boss quit, my bidet isn't working, it's just been a day. I need a charger. Traffic was nuts. I mean, was it nuts for you?

EILEEN. Not really. I rode my bike.

(*All serious.*) But something happened to me that *is* actually nuts.

ROBERT. What?

EILEEN. I got run over by a car.

---

* A license to produce *Inspired By True Events* does not include a performance license for any third-party or copyrighted music. Licensees should create an original composition or use music in the public domain. For further information, please see the Music and Third-Party Materials Use Note on page iii.

ROBERT. Tonight?

EILEEN. On my way here.

ROBERT. Are you okay?

EILEEN. I honestly should be in the ER.

ROBERT. Why aren't you?

EILEEN. Brett's insurance lapsed.

ROBERT. I'm glad you're not dead.

EILEEN. Can you imagine?

ROBERT. *(Charging his phone.)* There is so much going on outside. Ambulances and police cars. I didn't know Rochester had that many emergency vehicles. And, don't say it, "I embellish everything," blah, blah, blah, but this is *not* one of those times.

(From outside, a siren is heard.)

*(**EILEEN** opens the door and walks outside.)*

(Yelling off.) See?

EILEEN. *(Offstage.)* I see nothing.

ROBERT. You don't see all the cops?

EILEEN. Nope.

*(**ROBERT** heads outside.)*

(Beat.)

Oh, wait, yes. Now I *do* see a cop.

ROBERT. *(Offstage.)* There was more of them further North. There were even helicopters.

EILEEN. Really?

ROBERT. Yes! I've never seen anything like it.

EILEEN. Did you check Twitter?

ROBERT. I was suspended from Twitter.

>(**EILEEN** *enters, looking on her phone.* **ROBERT** *follows behind.*)

I have lived in Rochester my whole life, and I've never seen helicopters so close to the ground. It's so war-like. I suddenly felt like I was Willem Dafoe at the end of *Platoon*.

(Dropping to his knees, arms up, crying.) Help me! They're gonna kill me! I'm gonna die! In Vietnam! Don't leave me here! Take me with you, please!

Ah!

>*(Beat.)*

EILEEN. That's not how *Platoon* ends.

ROBERT. I just watched the movie.

EILEEN. Willem Dafoe never said anything remotely close to that.

ROBERT. Come on, Eileen. Why won't you let me have any fun?

EILEEN. I'm sorry your bad Vietnam War re-enactment was un-fun.

ROBERT. You make me sound awful.

EILEEN. You are awful.

>*(A smile.)*

JK I love you.

>*(From the TV monitor, the murmur of the audience grows louder and louder.)*

ROBERT. *(Re: the monitor.)* Do we have an *actual* audience?

EILEEN. *(Gravely.)* Robert.

(Beat.)

EILEEN. We're sold out.

ROBERT. All one hundred and eighteen seats?

EILEEN. Yes. We are a hit.

ROBERT. *(Almost sad.)* Oh no. Really?

EILEEN. Yes! Didn't you read the reviews?

ROBERT. *(Plugging his ears.)* Ahhh. No, no, no. If you believe the good ones, you have to believe the bad ones.

(Beat.)

Did they say anything about me?

EILEEN. You just said you didn't want to know.

*(**ROBERT** says nothing.)*

They liked you.

ROBERT. *(Touching his toupee.)* Did they say anything bad?

EILEEN. No.

ROBERT. *(Almost sad.)* This is so exciting.

*(**ROBERT** pours a cup of coffee as **EILEEN** plugs in hot rollers.)*

(Beat.)

Where's my Colin?

EILEEN. He's not *your* Colin.

ROBERT. He's my boo-thing.

EILEEN. Your husband would be so pissed if he heard you.

ROBERT. Bruce'd tell me to slap handcuffs on that gorgeous man-candy and toss him in the sling.

EILEEN. Gross.

ROBERT. Don't kink shame.

EILEEN. He's in the dressing room. He and Claire broke up.

ROBERT. Oh no. Is he okay?

EILEEN. Mary thinks he's being weird so she's considering cancelling.

ROBERT. She can't do that.

EILEEN. J'agree.

ROBERT. Oh man. He loved Claire.

EILEEN. Yeah. But, honestly, if I'm lucky, she'll be too sad to live in Rochester now and I won't have to compete with her for parts.

ROBERT. I know it's a tricky concept to wrap your head around, but this is not about you.

EILEEN. Oh, don't feign concern. Now you can objectify him without competition.

(Reading from her phone.) Ugh. There's nothing. Rochester needs to step it up with their city gossip.

(Worried, looking up.) Oh, no.

ROBERT. What?

EILEEN. This man today. The guy who hit me. He was giving Charles Manson. What if *he* did something?

ROBERT. Really?

EILEEN. I'm telling you. Something's off.

(The intercom comes on.)

CHRISTINA. *(Offstage, from the intercom.)* Good evening. Hi Robert. We got your / text.

MARY. *(From the intercom, side-coaching.)* Tell him about being on / time.

CHRISTINA. We want to remind you, Robert, that you are not excused from / half hour.

MARY. That's / great.

CHRISTINA. You need to be on time, just like the rest of your / cast.

ROBERT. *(Yelling to the intercom.)* There was traffic, Christina!

CHRISTINA. If you haven't signed in yet, please do / so now.

MARY. Say five minutes / again.

CHRISTINA. This is your five minute call / everybody.

ROBERT & EILEEN. Thank you / five.

MARY. That's great / Christina.

CHRISTINA. Five minutes till top of show. Five minutes.

(The intercom goes off, loudly.)

ROBERT. I want a later call. We still have like forty minutes before we even step onstage.

*(**ROBERT** goes to the sign-in sheet.)*

(Re: sign-in stickers.) Ooo. *Friends* stickers for sign-in. I'mma be Chandler.

EILEEN. *(As Janice from* Friends.*)* Oh gawd. Look at you. Such a Chandler Bing. Hehehehe.

(Beat.)

(Melancholy.) Ugh, it's so sad he died.

ROBERT. I know. I loved him.

*(**COLIN** enters into the green room, dressed as a mechanic. He's a little off, but generally okay.)*

COLIN. Five minutes till places.

(Hugging **EILEEN**.*)* Eileen.

(Hugging **ROBERT**.*)* Robert.

(Beat.)

(Trying his best.) I am so psyched about the show. I have a friend here. She's an ex, but we're cool. God, I am so fucking proud of our play.

*(***MARY** *walks into the green room.)*

MARY. Hi, Robert. Thanks for joining us.

ROBERT. It wasn't my fault.

COLIN. Hey Mary – up top.

(High-fiving.) I know, I'm at places in like three, I know. I cannot wait!

(To **EILEEN** *and* **ROBERT**, *tender.)* We're lifting this huge fucking boulder, *as a team*, and if one of us isn't ready, then it all falls apart. I'm gonna do so good tonight. Don't you worry.

(To **MARY**, *serious.)* Thank you. For earlier.

MARY. Of course, honey.

COLIN. I napped. Took a shower. I smell better.

(To **EILEEN** *and* **ROBERT**.*)* Every night, when you guys are onstage, I sit in the green room and cry.

(Kinda emotional.) You're the best part of our play.

ROBERT. That's nice of you, Colin.

EILEEN. Thank you.

COLIN. *(Pumping himself up.)* Fuck yeah. Let's do / this!

CHRISTINA. *(Offstage, from the intercom.)* Colin, it's your places call. Places for the top of show. / Places please. Thank you.

COLIN. *(A bit unhinged.)* Thank you, places. Ahhh! Let's do this. Let's fucking *do this*!!!

(**EILEEN** and **ROBERT** *share a look. Odd.*)

(*The* **CAST** *huddles up, grounding themselves.*)

COLIN, EILEEN & ROBERT. *(Genuinely.)* I got your back, I got your back, I got your back...

(*Deep, communal breath. An exhale.*)

(*Then,* **COLIN** *rushes to the stage. He turns back.*)

COLIN. Fuck 'em in the heart, y'all. Fuck 'em in the heart.

(**COLIN** *leaves the green room.*)

ROBERT. *(Beat.)* He'll be fine.

EILEEN. I'm sure he gobbled up one of his eighty medications and is happy we're sold out.

MARY. Well, I'm glad you both feel okay because I haven't heard back from Todd.

EILEEN. I can't believe we need Todd's permission to cancel. I hate him. Todd's cancelled. Let's cancel Todd.

ROBERT. He shouldn't be calling the shots. You should be, Mary.

EILEEN. J'agree. I'm revoking his Evite to my birthday party.

ROBERT. What birthday party?

MARY. *(Looking at watch.)* I'm gonna go to the booth to be with Christina for top of show.

EILEEN. All right.

MARY. Have a great time, guys.

EILEEN. We will.

ROBERT. Thanks.

> (**MARY** *leaves.*)
>
> (*On the TV monitor, pre-show music begins.**)

EILEEN. Mary needs to stand up to Todd, don't you think?

ROBERT. Yes.

EILEEN. (*Grabbing her phone.*) Okay. I'm setting our alarm for thirty minutes.

ROBERT. Thank you, thirty.

> (**EILEEN** *sets an alarm on her phone. She checks her hot rollers and begins putting them into her hair, getting ready for the show.*)
>
> (*Then –*)

When is your birthday party?

EILEEN. Thursday. I sent you an Evite.

ROBERT. You did? I didn't get it.

EILEEN. Check your junk mail.

> (**ROBERT** *goes to his phone and scrolls.*)
>
> (*On the TV monitor, the house lights dim. The audience applauds politely.*)

ROBERT. (*Sad, worried.*) Listen to that. We're packed.

EILEEN. Sh. Sh. I want to hear my pre-show announcement.

ROBERT. (*Looking at his phone.*) There's nothing in my junk mail about your birthday party.

---

* A license to produce *Inspired By True Events* does not include a performance license for any third-party or copyrighted music. Licensees should create an original composition or use music in the public domain. For further information, please see the Music and Third-Party Materials Use Note on page iii.

EILEEN. Sh, sh, sh.

> (**ROBERT** and **EILEEN** hover in front of the TV monitor. From the auditorium, we hear **EILEEN**'s pre-recorded pre-show announcement.)

EILEEN'S RECORDED VOICE. *(Through the intercom, actor-y voice.)* Thank you for coming to The Uptown Theatre. We are thrilled you chose to spend your evening with us. Please take this time to silence all cell phones and open any candy wrappers.

> *(The audience laughs.)*

EILEEN. Why is that funny to people?

EILEEN'S RECORDED VOICE. For the sake of your fellow audience members, and the actors performing onstage, please refrain from talking, texting, and eating during the performance. Thanks again for spending your evening with us, and enjoy the show.

> *(The audience claps. The show begins.)*

> *(Bolded text indicates dialogue and action occurring on the TV monitor.)*

ANNOUNCEMENT. **The following story you're about to witness is inspired by true events. Any resemblance to actual persons, living or dead, or actual events is purely coincidental.**

> *(Murmurs from the **CROWD**.)*

> (**COLIN** *walks onto the stage. He stands under a single spotlight. He's an excellent actor.*)

COLIN. **When I was sixteen, my driver's license had a misprint on it. My address was off by a single digit. When I was sixteen, a man stole my wallet. That**

same man broke into the house that he thought was mine. He was looking for me. But, he found someone else.

EILEEN. He's so good at acting.

ROBERT. I know. Such a DiCaprio.

COLIN. I now live in Wilmington, Delaware. Working a lifeless job that has nothing to do with my degree. The only prerequisite I had for moving was that I'd get as far from Valdosta as I could get; as far from my parents; as far from my shame; as far from… him.

> (**ROBERT** *turns the volume down.*)

EILEEN. See, it's Val-DAH-sta – not Val-DOO-sta.

> (**ROBERT** *stares at her.*)

Just pronounce it correctly.

> (**COLIN's** *performance continues to play on the TV monitor.*)
>
> (**ROBERT** *grabs some black powder and a small hand mirror. He begins applying the powder to his face, making himself look dirty.*)
>
> (*Suddenly, that weird scratching sound is back.*)

EILEEN. *(Startled.)* Oh god!

ROBERT. What the hell was that?!

EILEEN. The mice. They're back.

ROBERT. No.

EILEEN. There is probably a mound of dead ones rotting away in the wall.

ROBERT. Gross. Stop, stop, stop.

EILEEN. That's what happened last time. They'd been piled for weeks.

ROBERT. Should we check?

EILEEN. God, no.

ROBERT. Then I will.

> (**ROBERT** *finds a screwdriver in a drawer. He then grabs a prop sword from the prop closet.*)

EILEEN. *(Re: the sword.)* Is that necessary?

ROBERT. We can skewer them.

EILEEN. That's actually smart.

ROBERT. Thank you.

> (**ROBERT** *heads to the wall. He bends down, looking through the vent.*)

EILEEN. See anything?

ROBERT. No. Not really.

(Grabbing the screwdriver.) All right... Let me just...

> (**ROBERT** *unscrews the screen from the vent.*)

EILEEN. Oh, wait, actually, wait. We should put up a barricade. In case the mice run out. We can trap them, or whatever.

ROBERT. Good. Let's do that.

> (*They hunt around the green room, grabbing anything that's stackable and wall-like.*)

EILEEN. Hey Robert, do you mind not stepping into my light during our first big exchange?

ROBERT. What first big exchange?

EILEEN. When we're talking about the murder. I feel upstaged. And if you're physically moving while I'm talking, then the audience is gonna think the moment is about you.

>   (**ROBERT** *just stares at her.*)

When you change Tina's staging, I panic and skip lines.

ROBERT. How is that my fault?

EILEEN. Just don't move on my lines.

ROBERT. Fine. Got any more notes?

EILEEN. Would you take them if I gave them to you?

ROBERT. Would you take mine if I gave them to you?

EILEEN. If they were good.

>   (**EILEEN** *grabs a blanket.*)

ROBERT. What's the blanket for?

EILEEN. To catch any spillovers.

>   (*They complete a semi-circle in front of the vent.*)

That should do it.

ROBERT. Unless they're climbers.

EILEEN. Don't even.

>   (**ROBERT** *unscrews the vent and pulls off the screen.*)

(*Suddenly terrified.*) Ah! Oh shit!

ROBERT. (*Equally terrified.*) What, what, what?!

EILEEN. I thought I saw something.

ROBERT. Don't do that. You scared the shit out of me.

EILEEN. Sorry, sorry.

(**ROBERT** *pokes his head inside the vent.*)

Careful.

ROBERT. I am being very careful.

EILEEN. Do you see anything?

ROBERT. No, but ugh. It smells horrible.

EILEEN. What does it smell like?

ROBERT. I don't know. It's pungent.

EILEEN. Gross.

(**ROBERT** *reaches for the sword.*)

ROBERT. M'lady.

(**EILEEN** *grabs the sword.*)

EILEEN. Handing the sword.

(*They laugh as she ceremonially passes it to him.* **ROBERT** *looks around inside the vent.*)

(*Beat.*)

EILEEN. See anything?

ROBERT. Oh, wait, yes. There is, like... I don't know.

EILEEN. Do you need a light?

ROBERT. No, no. Like, maybe it's a costume piece or something. I can't really reach it. And, oh...

EILEEN. What?

ROBERT. There are these little black things.

EILEEN. What do you mean?

ROBERT. It's everywhere.

EILEEN. Like mice droppings?

ROBERT. Yeah, maybe. I think so. Looks like it to me.

EILEEN. Ugh. Gross.

ROBERT. I don't know.

> *(Beat.)*

Ugh. I'm not sticking my head all the way in.

(Waving his hands at the vent.) I'm just gonna leave this for Mary to deal with.

> **(ROBERT** *doesn't restore the cover to the vent. He ceremonially hands* **EILEEN** *the sword.)*

EILEEN. Receiving the sword.

> **(ROBERT** *rolls his eyes, charmed.* **EILEEN** *puts the sword away.)*

If I hear the mice tomorrow, *I'm* cancelling the show. Todd can suck it.

> **(EILEEN** *turns the TV monitor's volume up.)*

COLIN. *(Slowly.)* We had to verify our contact info with our driver's training instructor. Address, phone number, place of birth. My actual address was 1657 Crenshaw.

> *(Long beat.)*

The DMV accidentally printed 1652 Crenshaw.

> *(Longer beat.)*

7... 2.

> *(Longest beat.)*

My license was off by a single digit. He went to the wrong house. Because of me. He murdered someone else. Because of me. That death was on my hands.

(**EILEEN** *mutes the TV.*)

EILEEN. *(Rolling her eyes.)* Someone read his reviews.

(*Silence falls.*)

Oh, so last night, you know the section when we pull up to the house, and I usually scream, but I didn't?

ROBERT. Is this another note?

EILEEN. No. But do you remember me not screaming?

ROBERT. Yes.

EILEEN. Well, I got thrown because I thought I heard someone's cell phone vibrating. It was happening throughout that whole section. Did you hear it?

ROBERT. No.

EILEEN. Well, I almost lost it – until I looked into the audience and realized that there was an older man on a breathing machine. Someone needs to let us know if we have a patron like that. I suddenly got so angry at Mary. Can you remind me to say something to her?

ROBERT. Sure.

(*They grab their costumes from the laundry pile.*)

Thanks for doing this.

EILEEN. You bet.

ROBERT. Got anyone here tonight?

EILEEN. My mom. I haven't seen her since my wedding.

(*Beat.*)

What about you?

ROBERT. My brother.

EILEEN. I didn't know you had a brother.

ROBERT. He lives out of state. His name is Bert, but when he meets you he'll probably introduce himself as "Glenn" or "Clint". He's insane. I would say, "Eileen, have you met my brother *Bert*?" And you'd be totally confused because that's probably not the name he gave you. I love him, but if I seem off, I'm apologizing now.

> (**ROBERT** *collects his costume from the wardrobe rack. He goes into the dressing room.* **EILEEN** *grabs her costume and heads to the bathroom.*)

(*Offstage.*) Ew.

EILEEN. (*Offstage.*) What?

ROBERT. It smells in here, too.

EILEEN. Gross.

ROBERT. Yeah. Something's rotting.

EILEEN. Turn on the fan.

> (*From inside the dressing room,* **ROBERT** *tries to turn on a fan.*)
>
> (*Beat.*)

ROBERT. It doesn't work. Figures.

> (*Silence as they both put on their costumes.*)
>
> (*Then,* **ROBERT** *tries to open a window.*)

Ugh. Todd needs to fix these windows. There needs to be some air flow.

> (*More silence as they get dressed.*)
>
> (*Then –*)

Ugh. Come smell this.

EILEEN. I will not be doing that.

> *(More silence.)*

> *(Then –)*

ROBERT. Did nobody empty the trash?

> *(Silence.)*

> *(They do vocal warm-ups as they complete their changes.)*

> *(Then –)*

What is that?

EILEEN. What?

ROBERT. Is this yours?

EILEEN. I don't know what you're looking at.

ROBERT. The bag.

EILEEN. What bag?

ROBERT. Come here.

EILEEN. Ugh.

> *(**EILEEN** leaves the bathroom and heads to the dressing room. She peeks inside.)*

(Offstage.) Ew.

ROBERT. Told you. Is that yours?

EILEEN. It's probably Colin's. God only knows what he put in there.

ROBERT. He needs to not keep shit in here. There's no room.

(Gagging.) Ew. It's definitely this. I'm just gonna get it out of here.

(From inside the dressing room, the sound of a bag being dragged.)

EILEEN. Careful. Don't throw out your back.

(Beat.)

I'm not being ageist. You have filled out accident reports on all three of our last shows.

ROBERT. Michael slammed the hilt of his dagger into my rib cage. That wasn't my fault.

EILEEN. I never said it was your fault, just be careful.

*(**ROBERT** enters, pulling a large duffel bag into the green room.)*

*(**MARY** walks in.)*

MARY. *(Looking at watch.)* Hey, you two are roughly at a ten now.

ROBERT & EILEEN. Thank you, ten.

MARY. Colin's doing great. A little slow, but I'm just –

(Re: the bag.) What's that?

ROBERT. He needs to not keep his rank gym clothes at the theatre. Can we put this outside?

MARY. No.

ROBERT. It smells awful.

EILEEN. *(Under her breath.)* It smells like ass.

MARY. *(Inhaling.)* Ew, wow.

ROBERT. See? Let's put it in the parking lot.

*(**EILEEN** grabs air freshener and sprays it everywhere.)*

Okay, okay. I think we're good. Now it smells like B.O. and lemons.

EILEEN. I'd rather be inhaling this than whatever *that* is.

MARY. *(Noticing something.)* Oh, no.

ROBERT. What?

MARY. It's leaking. If you guys broke something, I swear to god.

ROBERT. What?

MARY. Just – be respectful.

(Rubbing fingers together.) Ew. It's sticky.

EILEEN. Really? Gross.

MARY. *(Stunned.)* I think this is blood.

> *(Stunned silence.)*
>
> *(Nobody moves.)*
>
> *(You could hear a pin drop.)*
>
> *(Then –)*

ROBERT. Did you say blood?

MARY. Yeah.

(Holding up a red finger.) This looks like blood.

> *(Beat.)*

Are you sure this is Colin's bag?

ROBERT. I think so.

EILEEN. It's definitely not mine.

MARY. Has anybody else been in the dressing room?

EILEEN. I don't know.

ROBERT. Maybe someone went in during the party.

> *(**MARY** slowly takes a peek into the bag.)*

EILEEN. What are you doing?

MARY. Just having a look.

EILEEN. Why?

MARY. To make sure it's his.

> *(She slowly zips open the bag and pulls out a single item. It's wrapped in a towel and secured with duct tape. It's also soaked in blood.)*

EILEEN. *(Gasping.)* Oh my god.

ROBERT. *(Beat.)* What is that?

> *(**MARY** grabs scissors from a drawer.)*

(Aside, to **EILEEN**.*)* Oh, oh – you wanted to tell Mary about the guy with the breathing machine.

EILEEN. Really, Robert? Right now?

ROBERT. I just thought of it.

> *(**MARY** cuts into the bloody, wrapped object.)*

EILEEN. Don't cut into it.

ROBERT. Why are you doing that?

MARY. Because... Because I just...

> *(**MARY** unrolls the wrapped object slowly.)*
>
> *(A dismembered human arm falls to the floor.)*
>
> *(They all freak out.)*

EILEEN. *(Screaming.)* AH!

ROBERT. AHH!!

MARY. SHH!!! There is a show going on!

EILEEN. I don't care.

ROBERT. What *is* that?

MARY. *(Matter of fact.)* I think it's an arm.

EILEEN. AH!

MARY. Sh. Quiet.

EILEEN. No. I will not be quiet.

>   *(Beat.)*

MARY. *(Sober.)* It's an arm.

>   *(Beat.)*

ROBERT. Is it a prop?

>   *(Beat.)*

MARY. No.

EILEEN. No, no, no.

>   (**EILEEN** *hides in the bathroom.*)

>   *(Beat.)*

MARY. Oh, wow.

>   *(Beat.)*

ROBERT. And that's *definitely* Colin's bag?

MARY. You said it was his bag.

ROBERT. How would I know, Mary?!

EILEEN. *(Offstage.)* Fuck.

>   *(Beat.)*

ROBERT. What do we do?

>   *(Beat.)*

MARY. I don't know.

EILEEN. *(Breathing heavily.)* This is bad.

ROBERT. That's a *human* arm, right?

    (Beat.)

MARY. *(Looking closely.)* Yes.

    (**EILEEN** *re-enters from the bathroom.*)

    (Beat.)

EILEEN. Is it real?

MARY. Yes.

    (Beat.)

ROBERT. Shit.

EILEEN. No, no, no.

    (Beat.)

MARY. Um.

ROBERT. Is there anything else?

    (**MARY** *kinda peeks inside the bag.*)

EILEEN. Careful.

MARY. I am.

    (Beat.)

Looks like more of the same.

EILEEN. Oh god.

    (Beat.)

MARY. *(Devastated.)* This is not good.

>   (**ROBERT**, **EILEEN**, *and* **MARY** *stand in silence for a while. A long, long, long while.*)
>
>   *(The shock is overwhelming.)*
>
>   *(Nobody knows what to say. What to do.)*

MARY. Um.

>   *(Beat.)*

Okay.

>   *(Beat.)*

Everyone. Um...

>   *(Beat.)*

We just need to relax.

EILEEN. Do not tell us to relax.

ROBERT. This is bad.

EILEEN. We need to call the police.

MARY. Just give me a second.

EILEEN. For what? Call the police.

MARY. I need a second to process this.

EILEEN. To process what?

>   (**MARY** *delicately puts the arm back into the bag.*)

Oh god.

ROBERT. Oh, no.

EILEEN. Stop touching it.

>   (**MARY** *zips the bag shut. She's overwhelmed.*)

(After an epic silence...)

MARY. Okay. Um.

(Beat.)

Lemme – okay.

(Beat, complete resolve.)

This is what we're gonna do.

*(**MARY** exhales.)*

(Beat, crystal clarity.)

We're gonna finish our show.

EILEEN. Ah, no. We are not.

ROBERT. You're joking.

EILEEN. I'm not getting on the stage. No fucking way.

MARY. You're gonna have to.

EILEEN. Ah, no. I'm gonna "have to" call the police is what I'm gonna "have to" do.

MARY. I will call the police.

EILEEN. When?

MARY. Once you two are onstage.

EILEEN. Ah, no. You and Colin are way too – no, no.

ROBERT. We should stop the show.

MARY. If we stop it before the police get here, then Colin will wanna know why we stopped. As will the hundred or so audience members. He might freak out.

EILEEN. Just say we were having a technical problem.

MARY. I don't think we should do that.

EILEEN. You're a stage manager, not a police person. You're not qualified to make decisions like this. I'm sorry, but no. I'm calling the police. This is ridiculous. Where's my phone? Does anyone see my phone?

ROBERT. *(Pointing to the counter.)* It's over there.

*(**EILEEN** goes to her phone.)*

MARY. Can you just give it a second, Eileen?

EILEEN. Nope, sorry. I cannot.

*(**EILEEN** starts dialing. **MARY** grabs the phone out of her hand.)*

MARY. Listen to me.

EILEEN. Give me my phone back, please.

MARY. We need to think about this.

EILEEN. Give me my phone back, Mary!

MARY. We could put people in danger.

EILEEN. Someone already *was* in danger!

ROBERT. I think Mary might be right.

EILEEN. How?

ROBERT. Honestly, the safest place for us probably *is* onstage.

EILEEN. You guys are fucked. I'm not being an accomplice to whatever the... I like... I can't breathe.

(Deep breaths.)

I think I'm having a panic attack.

*(**EILEEN** backs into the wardrobe rack, which startles her and causes her to scream even more.)*

Ahh!

MARY. If we stop the show before the police get here, then he could... You guys, please. Colin's gonna be down here any second. We need / to –

>   *(Suddenly, muffled gunshots are heard in the distance.)*

ROBERT. What the fuck was / that?

>   *(Terrified,* **ROBERT** *and* **EILEEN** *look at the TV monitor.)*

EILEEN. Colin has a / gun!

ROBERT. Oh my / god!

MARY. *(Keeping it cool.)* It's the *prop* gun. It's just the gun in the play. It's the prop.

EILEEN. *(Relief.)* Oh right.

ROBERT. Oh thank god.

MARY. It was just the sound cue. It doesn't even work. That's all it was.

>   *(A group exhale.)*
>
>   *(Then –)*

EILEEN. *(Grave.)* Oh no. Oh, Robert.

ROBERT. What?

EILEEN. *(Mortified.)* Do you think all those helicopters were looking for Colin?

MARY. What helicopters?

ROBERT. It doesn't seem possible. He's not...

>   *(A loss for words, then –)*

Maybe he didn't pack the bag. Maybe someone is making him carry it.

EILEEN. Sorry, but no – I can't have this right now.

(**EILEEN** *heads to her bike.*)

MARY. Eileen, wait.

EILEEN. Fuck this.

MARY. Please / wait.

EILEEN. No!

(*The intercom chaotically comes on.*)

CHRISTINA. (*Offstage, from the intercom.*) Hey, Robert and Eileen? Colin skipped almost an entire page. Your entrance is coming up quick. Please head to the stage immediately. Thank you.

(*Everyone looks at the monitor.* **ROBERT** *quickly turns the volume up.*)

COLIN. (***Confessing.***) **I had assumed I was invincible. His death was all my fault. I'm to blame. It's me. ME!!**

EILEEN. (*To the TV.*) EXACTLY!

(**ROBERT** *mutes the TV.*)

MARY. You guys –

(*Firm and controlled.*) I don't want to make a mistake.

EILEEN. You *are* making a mistake! *This* is a / mistake!

CHRISTINA. (*Offstage, from the intercom.*) Hurry up. Thank you.

MARY. Please, Eileen. If Colin comes in here – and we're all just standing around – what do you think he is gonna do?

(*Silence.*)

Didn't you say your mother was here?

EILEEN. Don't do that, Mary.

MARY. Do you want something bad to happen to her?

EILEEN. Of course not!

MARY. Then we gotta act like we didn't find this so that nothing escalates!

(Silence.)

EILEEN. Fuck this.

*(With that, **EILEEN** parks her bike.)*

I need to see you dial.

MARY. Really?

EILEEN. I need to *see* you dial and *hear* you talk to the police and then I will go. But you need to do it right now. RIGHT. FUCKING. NOW.

*(**MARY** picks up her phone and dials.)*

ROBERT. What do we do when it's over?

MARY. If they don't stop the show, just take your bow and leave with the audience. Find your family and get out of the building.

ROBERT. What are you going to do?

MARY. I'll be fine.

EILEEN. Is 911 not picking up?

MARY. No. It's just / ringing.

(The intercom comes on.)

CHRISTINA. *(Offstage, from the intercom.)* Hey Mary. What do / I do?

MARY. You guys, / please.

EILEEN. Still no answer?

MARY. No. It's a bad / connection, but I'll keep trying.

EILEEN. *(Heading to the door.)* Fucking Rochester! This is such bull/shit!!

ROBERT. *(Heading to the door.)* Be careful, Mary.

> *(EILEEN and ROBERT quickly head to the stage.)*
>
> *(Once gone, MARY hangs up the phone. She clearly never dialed. She stares at the phone, her head drops.)*
>
> ***(On the TV monitor, COLIN leaves the stage as EILEEN and ROBERT enter it. They stand under two spotlights. They begin their part of the play.)***
>
> *(Down in the green room, MARY is alone. Terrified.)*
>
> *(After a moment, COLIN frantically enters the green room.)*

COLIN. Fuck! You're better than that, Colin. You blew it. You / fucking blew it.

MARY. Shhh. Shhh. There is a show going on!

> *(COLIN stops cold when he sees his bag in the center of the room.)*

(Quick thinking.) The dressing rooms are too small for storing larger personal items. You know better.

(Silence.)

Next time, send me a text so I can help you find a better place.

(Silence.)

(**COLIN** *looks at* **MARY**.)

(*For a long while.*)

(*Then –*)

COLIN. (*Saving face.*) I skipped five minutes of the play. Maybe more.

MARY. Well, you shoulda looked at your script, honey. You're not as young as you used to be. You gotta be more professional.

(*Suddenly, Eileen's phone alarm goes off.*)

(*Jumpy.*) Oh lord have mercy.

(*Beat.*)

I forgot they set an alarm.

(**MARY** *turns off the alarm.*)

COLIN. I was trying to remember what I'd skipped, so I could insert it back in, but I couldn't even think of a place. The audience is not gonna be able to follow the fucking plot.

(**COLIN** *turns the volume up on the TV.*)

(**On the monitor, ROBERT** *and* **EILEEN** *perform their part of the play.*)

ROBERT. I was worried we'd never find something affordable in...

(*Hesitates.*)

...Valdosta. But it was too good a job to pass on. We needed a change.

EILEEN. I had no idea he'd even been offered this job, let alone accepted. He never tells me anything.

ROBERT. The future was ours.

EILEEN. It was the worst day of my life. At the time, I was six weeks pregnant.

ROBERT. We were six weeks pregnant.

EILEEN. The baby wasn't his. He still doesn't know.

ROBERT. Stealing began as a means to an end. A credit card here, a wallet there.

EILEEN. I found handguns. In his drawer. He owned like seven.

ROBERT. Everything was going fine.

(Beat.)

Until the night I broke into that man's house.

*(**COLIN** turns the volume down.)*

*(**EILEEN** and **ROBERT**'s performance continues to play on the TV monitor.)*

COLIN. We should stop.

MARY. Why?

COLIN. The audience is going to be confused. We should give them a full / refund –

(The intercom comes on.)

CHRISTINA. *(Offstage, from the intercom.)* Mary?

*(**MARY** gets startled.)*

Can you come up to the booth? I have a quick question. Thank you.

(Beat.)

COLIN. *(Taking her in.)* You okay?

MARY. It's Christina with that damn intercom.

> (**MARY** *grabs her walkie.*)

(Into the walkie.) Christina?

> *(Beat.)*

Christina?

> *(Waits.)*

She's not answering. It's better for her training anyway if she figures it out / on her own –

> *(The intercom comes on, loudly.)*

CHRISTINA. *(Offstage, from the intercom.)* Mary, please get up here as soon as you can. Eileen just skipped. I don't know what's happening, but she's a mess. Thank you.

COLIN. Let's stop.

MARY. *(Into the walkie.)* Christina?

> *(Beat.)*

Her walkie must be dead.

> *(Beat.)*

I'll be right back.

> (**MARY** *leaves the green room.*)

> (**COLIN** *is alone. He stares at his bag. Frozen. He looks at the vent.*)

> (*After a few moments,* **MARY** *returns. She watches* **COLIN** *staring at the vent.*)

See anything?

(**COLIN** *stands.*)

MARY. Eileen skipped a few lines, but nothing major, and poor Christina wasn't sure where to call the cue, but we picked a good spot.

(*Unsure of what to do,* **MARY** *pours coffee.*)

Need a cup?

(*Silence falls.*)

(*Then –*)

Um...

(*Beat.*)

(*Tactic change.*)

You know what I've been thinking?

(*Beat.*)

It's actually something that I have never told you.

(*Keeping things light.*) Do you know I was with your mother when she found out she was pregnant with you?

(*Beat.*)

COLIN. Why are you talking about my mom?

MARY. I guess seeing Eileen in her pregnant belly made me think of it.

(*Beat.*)

(*Laser focus.*) So, your mom was babysitting me – I was maybe eight or nine – and I went with her to the drugstore on Sycamore. I could tell she was nervous, but I didn't know what was going on. Later, I was in her bathroom and I saw this thing in the trash can.

> *(A smile.)*

A pregnancy test.

> *(Beat.)*

She was so happy. All she ever wanted was to be a mother.

> *(Silence.)*
>
> *(Then, **COLIN** laughs.)*

Why is that funny?

COLIN. I don't want to talk about my mom.

MARY. Okay.

COLIN. She sucks.

> **(MARY** *checks her phone, trying to act normal.)*
>
> *(Then –)*

MARY. *(Delicate.)* Have you talked to Claire?

COLIN. We broke up.

MARY. I wasn't sure if she tried to reach out. Just curious.

> **(COLIN** *laughs, to himself.)*

What's so funny?

COLIN. *(Mumbled, to himself.)* I didn't think she'd scream.

> **(MARY** *hears this, very concerned.)*
>
> *(Beat.)*

Maybe I should still propose.

MARY. Really?

(Beat.)

COLIN. *(A thought.)* Guess it depends.

MARY. On what?

(Beat.)

COLIN. *(A mumble.)* Jonathan.

MARY. What was that, honey?

COLIN. Jonathan. My neighbor. I needed money from him.

MARY. *(Nodding.)* Right. For Claire's ring.

*(**COLIN** looks at **MARY**. Like, really looks at her. It's scary.)*

(Beat.)

(Uncomfortable.) What?

COLIN. *(Beat.)* She was fucking Jonathan.

MARY. Oh.

(Beat.)

I'm sorry.

(Beat.)

When did you find out?

*(**COLIN** doesn't respond.)*

(Beat.)

If you knew Claire was cheating on you, why would you want to propose?

*(Out of discomfort, **COLIN** laughs.)*

COLIN. I don't feel good.

MARY. Do you need to lie down?

COLIN. I might throw up.

> (**COLIN** *looks at* **MARY**, *clearly at a loss.*)

MARY. Do you need the bathroom?

(An offering.) If you'd like to skip curtain call, and sleep at my apartment, I'd be okay with that.

> *(Beat.)*

COLIN. Um.

> *(Beat.)*

My ex is here.

MARY. Okay.

COLIN. I... um...

> *(Beat.)*

Don't be mad.

MARY. Why would I be?

COLIN. I... ah...

> *(Beat, a few breaths.)*

This kid who comes to our shows. He comes to all our shows.

MARY. Which kid?

COLIN. He stole Jonathan's ATM card.

MARY. So you *did* get the money?

COLIN. Yes.

MARY. I'm confused.

> (**COLIN** *breathes deeply.*)

COLIN. I don't know what I'm saying.

> *(Acutely aware of time, **MARY** turns on the TV monitor to see where they are in the show.)*

EILEEN. *(Panicking, losing her place.)* I should've paid attention. Ahhh. I should've noticed the signs. I don't know how I could've missed the signs. I was distracted.

> *(Dropping accent, almost for real.)* I'm distracted. I'm... I'm...

> *(Picking up the accent again.)* I blame myself. I was inconsolable. I gave my... / my...

ROBERT. *(Mumbling, feeding line.)* Baby up for adoption.

EILEEN. Baby up for adoption!! Ah!!! I thought I was incapable. He was the incapable one. Not me. It was him! HIM!!!!

> *(**MARY** turns off the TV monitor.)*

MARY. Colin...

> *(Beat.)*

Which kid are you talking about?

COLIN. Kyle Marks.

> *(**MARY** assumes the worst.)*

MARY. *(Quiet, devastated.)* Julie and Albert's Kyle?

COLIN. Yeah.

MARY. Okay.

> *(Beat.)*

Um.

(Beat.)

So, Kyle Marks stole Jonathan's ATM card? For you?

> *(**COLIN** says nothing.)*

You could've borrowed money from me.

> *(Silence.)*

COLIN. I, ah...

> *(Long silence.)*

I should give Jonathan his money back.

MARY. You'd feel better.

> *(Beat.)*

And, ah... Where is Kyle now?

> *(**COLIN** doesn't say anything. **MARY** gets her cell phone.)*

I'm just gonna give Julie and Albert a call.

COLIN. *(A tinge of evil.)* Don't.

> *(This sends a shiver up **MARY**'s spine.)*
>
> *(Long silence.)*

Last night... I was getting out of my car... Jonathan called me over.

> *(Beat.)*

He confronted me.

> *(Beat.)*

In his apartment.

> *(Beat.)*

MARY. *(Very delicate.)* And, um, where is Jonathan now?

COLIN. *(Snapping.) I don't know!!!*

>(**MARY** *backs up, utterly shaken.*)

MARY. *(Quietly horrified.)* Okay. Okay.

COLIN. Sorry.

MARY. Don't hurt me.

>*(Beat, trying.)*

Colin?

>*(Beat, tentative.)*

Can I ask you something?

>*(Beat, then –)*

What's in your bag?

>(**COLIN** *says nothing. Nobody moves. It's almost a stand-off.*)
>
>*(Long silence.)*
>
>*(Then –)*

I saw something.

>*(Beat.)*

COLIN. What?

MARY. *(Fragile.)* Blood.

>*(Beat.)*

On the zipper.

>*(Beat.)*

It was still wet.

(COLIN says nothing.)

This can stay between us.

(Beat.)

COLIN. Um.

(A mumble.)

I saw his body.

MARY. What?

COLIN. I saw his body.

(Beat.)

MARY. Whose?

COLIN. Um...

(Beat.)

MARY. Kyle's?

COLIN. No.

(Beat.)

Jonathan's.

(Beat.)

MARY. Dead?

COLIN. Yes.

*(**MARY** covers her mouth, trying to hold herself together.)*

(Beat.)

MARY. Okay.

(Beat.)

Do you know how he died?

COLIN. No.

(*Beat.*)

MARY. Okay.

(*Beat.*)

Is Kyle dead?

COLIN. No.

MARY. Oh, thank god.

(*Beat.*)

Did you call the police?

(*Beat.*)

COLIN. I didn't kill Jonathan.

(*Beat.*)

MARY. You were in his apartment?

(*Silence.*)

Did you touch him?

(*Silence.*)

COLIN. (*Deep, long breaths.*) I remember the sound. Not doing it. Just... the sound.

(*Beat.*)

It was heavy.

(*Beat.*)

And then I was holding it – *his head* – like it had always been in my hand.

(**COLIN** *exhales.*)

MARY. *(Barely audible.)* Oh my god.

COLIN. I panicked.

MARY. I'm sure.

COLIN. I put his head in my bag.

MARY. Oh my god.

COLIN. *(A sudden release.)* I put some of Claire in our high school parking lot. It's where we first met. I put some of her near the mall. It's where we had our first date. I wanted to leave her places that made her happy. All I wanted was for Claire to be happy. I ran out of time, so I put some of her in the vents.

MARY. Oh my god.

COLIN. I was trying to get rid of Jonathan, but then Claire showed up. I didn't know they were fucking. I stabbed her. She hurt me. I loved her, but she hurt me.

(Beat.)

Some girls think they're the center of the world.

(Silence.)

MARY. *(Looks at her watch.)* I, ah...

(Deep breaths.)

Let me see where we are in the show.

(**MARY** *turns up the TV monitor.*)

ROBERT. I stabbed him! I stabbed him so many times! I lost control!

(**MARY** *quickly mutes the TV.*)

(Beat.)

MARY. We're close.

> *(Beat.)*

Um...

(Through tears.) Why do you think you would've done this, honey?

> *(**COLIN** says nothing.)*

> *(Then –)*

COLIN. I used to think he was a monster. All the screaming.

> *(Beat.)*

He always made it my fault.

> *(Beat.)*

Claire looked at me like I was my dad.

> *(Beat.)*

She saw a monster, so I gave her one.

> *(Silence.)*

> *(Beat.)*

MARY. Um –

(Taking control.) This is what we're gonna do. When the play is over, you're gonna take your bow.

Just like you normally do. And then you're gonna come back to the green room. I'll have Eileen and Robert leave with the audience. Don't call anyone. Don't leave. Don't do anything. Just wait.

> *(Beat.)*

Once everyone is gone, once it's just you and me, I'll drive you / to Canada.

(The intercom frantically blasts on.)

CHRISTINA. *(Offstage, from the intercom.)* Hey, Robert just skipped a chunk of text. This is terrible. I don't know what's happening. We're close to curtain. Thank you.

(Beat.)

MARY. Just come right here after you bow.

COLIN. I have an ex here tonight. I need to say hi.

MARY. Skip it.

COLIN. Okay.

(Beat.)

MARY. You should get up there.

COLIN. Okay.

(Beat.)

I'm not a monster.

(Beat.)

MARY. I know.

(Beat.)

It just happened. We'll figure it out.

*(**COLIN** heads up to the stage.)*

*(Once alone, **MARY** exhales. She's a mess. She can barely do anything.)*

*(After a moment, **MARY** grabs her phone and heads to the stage.)*

(On the TV monitor, the final moments of the play are performed. The lights dim.)

(The intercom gets turned on and the sound of applause can be heard through the speakers.)

(On the TV monitor, EILEEN, ROBERT, and COLIN *bow*.)

(They leave the stage.)

(The applause crescendos.)

(After a few moments, on the TV monitor, the ACTORS come back onstage and take an awkward second bow.)

(COLIN, *almost proud, beams as the applause continues*.)

(Eventually, COLIN leaves the stage.)

(EILEEN *and* ROBERT *linger before leaving the stage, towards the audience*.)

(After a few moments, COLIN enters the green room.)

(He's alone.)

(Then, MARY enters. She's fragile. They both are.)

(Beat.)

MARY. *(A mess.)* Hey.

COLIN. Hey.

> *(Beat.)*

Do we leave now?

MARY. Um.

(Long beat.)

We should...

(Beat.)

COLIN. What?

MARY. I, ah –

*(**MARY** glances at her phone.)*

(Then –)

(Beat, a decision made.) I left my keys.

(Beat.)

In the booth.

COLIN. Oh, okay.

MARY. *(With difficulty.)* Just wait here.

(Beat.)

I'll take care of everything.

*(**MARY** quickly hugs **COLIN**. It's an emotional hug. She knows it will be her last.)*

*(**MARY** leaves the green room.)*

*(**COLIN** is alone.)*

(He paces, worried.)

(After a long time, bright lights flash through all windows.)

FEMALE COP. *(Offstage, through a megaphone.)* This is the Rochester Police Department. Come out with your hands up.

>   (**COLIN** *panics. He looks around, remembering the vent.*)
>
>   (*Silence.*)
>
>   (**COLIN** *grabs the duffel and begins to shove it into the vent. It doesn't fit. He opens it and pulls out the wrapped, bloody arm. He shoves it into the vent. He pulls out the bloody, wrapped head. He shoves it into the vent. He then shoves the whole bag into the vent.*)
>
>   (*Silence.*)

COLIN. *(Yelling off.)* Mary?

>   (*Silence.*)

MALE COP. *(Offstage.)* Come out with your hands up.

>   (*Silence.*)

MARY. *(Offstage, painfully hard to say.)* Colin?

>   (*Beat.*)

Come out here, honey.

>   (*Upon hearing her voice,* **COLIN** *stops. A resolve.*)
>
>   (*Beat.*)

COLIN. *(A decision, yelling offstage.)* Okay.

>   (*Beat.*)

I'm coming. I'm coming.

>   (**COLIN** *heads towards the door that leads outside.*)
>
>   (*The intercom blasts on.*)

CHRISTINA. *(Offstage, from the intercom.)* Thank you cast for a / wonderful Friday performance.

MALE COP. *(Offstage.)* Put your hands straight up / in the air!

COLIN. *(Offstage.)* I'm sorry. / I'm sorry!

> *(The metal door to the outside slams shut.)*
>
> *(From inside the vent, the sound of mice scurrying.)*

CHRISTINA. *(Offstage, from the intercom.)* Remember, tomorrow is a two show day. Half hour is at one-thirty. Make sure your laundry ends up in the basket. Eileen's taking it home again. And thank you for bearing with me tonight. It was a real pleasure calling the show. Now everyone get home safely. Goodnight.

> *(From inside the walls, the sounds of more mice scurrying.)*
>
> *(And then more. And more.)*
>
> *(And then, an infestation.)*

End of Play

www.ingramcontent.com/pod-product-compliance
Lightning Source LLC
Chambersburg PA
CBHW071839290426
44109CB00017B/1872